This book belongs to:

A

Name	Appointments			
	Date	Time	Service	Price

Address

Email
Phone
Birthday
Special Requirements

Notes

Name	Date	Time	Service	Price

Address

Email
Phone
Birthday
Special Requirements

Notes

A

Name	Appointments			
	Date	Time	Service	Price
Address				
Email				
Phone				
Birthday				
Special Requirements				
Notes				

Name	Date	Time	Service	Price
Address				
Email				
Phone				
Birthday				
Special Requirements				
Notes				

A

Name	Appointments			
	Date	Time	Service	Price
Address				
Email				
Phone				
Birthday				
Special Requirements				
Notes				

Name	Date	Time	Service	Price
Address				
Email				
Phone				
Birthday				
Special Requirements				
Notes				

A

Name	Appointments			
	Date	Time	Service	Price
Address				
Email				
Phone				
Birthday				
Special Requirements				
Notes				

Name	Date	Time	Service	Price
Address				
Email				
Phone				
Birthday				
Special Requirements				
Notes				

A

	Appointments			
Name	Date	Time	Service	Price
Address				
Email				
Phone				
Birthday				
Special Requirements				
Notes				

Name	Date	Time	Service	Price
Address				
Email				
Phone				
Birthday				
Special Requirements				
Notes				

A

Name	Appointments			
	Date	Time	Service	Price
Address				
Email				
Phone				
Birthday				
Special Requirements				
Notes				

Name	Date	Time	Service	Price
Address				
Email				
Phone				
Birthday				
Special Requirements				
Notes				

B

Name	Appointments			
	Date	Time	Service	Price
Address				
Email				
Phone				
Birthday				
Special Requirements				
Notes				

Name	Date	Time	Service	Price
Address				
Email				
Phone				
Birthday				
Special Requirements				
Notes				

B

Name	Appointments			
	Date	Time	Service	Price
Address				
Email				
Phone				
Birthday				
Special Requirements				
Notes				

Name	Date	Time	Service	Price
Address				
Email				
Phone				
Birthday				
Special Requirements				
Notes				

B

Name	Appointments			
	Date	Time	Service	Price
Address				
Email				
Phone				
Birthday				
Special Requirements				
Notes				

Name	Date	Time	Service	Price
Address				
Email				
Phone				
Birthday				
Special Requirements				
Notes				

B

Name	Appointments			
	Date	Time	Service	Price
Address				
Email				
Phone				
Birthday				
Special Requirements				
Notes				

Name	Date	Time	Service	Price
Address				
Email				
Phone				
Birthday				
Special Requirements				
Notes				

B

	Appointments			
Name	Date	Time	Service	Price
Address				
Email				
Phone				
Birthday				
Special Requirements				
Notes				

Name	Date	Time	Service	Price
Address				
Email				
Phone				
Birthday				
Special Requirements				
Notes				

B

	Appointments			
Name	Date	Time	Service	Price
Address				
Email				
Phone				
Birthday				
Special Requirements				
Notes				
Name	Date	Time	Service	Price
Address				
Email				
Phone				
Birthday				
Special Requirements				
Notes				

C

Name	Appointments			
	Date	Time	Service	Price
Address				
Email				
Phone				
Birthday				
Special Requirements				
Notes				

Name	Date	Time	Service	Price
Address				
Email				
Phone				
Birthday				
Special Requirements				
Notes				

C

Name	Appointments			
	Date	Time	Service	Price
Address				
Email				
Phone				
Birthday				
Special Requirements				
Notes				

Name	Date	Time	Service	Price
Address				
Email				
Phone				
Birthday				
Special Requirements				
Notes				

C

Name	Appointments			
	Date	Time	Service	Price
Address				
Email				
Phone				
Birthday				
Special Requirements				
Notes				

Name	Date	Time	Service	Price
Address				
Email				
Phone				
Birthday				
Special Requirements				
Notes				

C

Name	Appointments			
	Date	Time	Service	Price
Address				
Email				
Phone				
Birthday				
Special Requirements				
Notes				

Name	Date	Time	Service	Price
Address				
Email				
Phone				
Birthday				
Special Requirements				
Notes				

C

	Appointments			
Name	Date	Time	Service	Price
Address				
Email				
Phone				
Birthday				
Special Requirements				
Notes				

Name	Date	Time	Service	Price
Address				
Email				
Phone				
Birthday				
Special Requirements				
Notes				

C

Name	Appointments			
	Date	Time	Service	Price
Address				
Email				
Phone				
Birthday				
Special Requirements				
Notes				

Name	Date	Time	Service	Price
Address				
Email				
Phone				
Birthday				
Special Requirements				
Notes				

D

Name	Appointments			
	Date	Time	Service	Price

Address

Email
Phone
Birthday
Special Requirements

Notes

Name	Date	Time	Service	Price

Address

Email
Phone
Birthday
Special Requirements

Notes

D

Name	Appointments			
	Date	Time	Service	Price
Address				
Email				
Phone				
Birthday				
Special Requirements				
Notes				

Name	Date	Time	Service	Price
Address				
Email				
Phone				
Birthday				
Special Requirements				
Notes				

D

Name	Appointments			
	Date	Time	Service	Price

Address

Email
Phone
Birthday
Special Requirements

Notes

Name	Date	Time	Service	Price

Address

Email
Phone
Birthday
Special Requirements

Notes

D

Name	Appointments			
	Date	Time	Service	Price
Address				
Email				
Phone				
Birthday				
Special Requirements				
Notes				

Name	Date	Time	Service	Price
Address				
Email				
Phone				
Birthday				
Special Requirements				
Notes				

D

Name		Appointments			
		Date	Time	Service	Price
Address					
Email					
Phone					
Birthday					
Special Requirements					
Notes					

Name		Date	Time	Service	Price
Address					
Email					
Phone					
Birthday					
Special Requirements					
Notes					

D

Name	Appointments			
	Date	Time	Service	Price

Address

Email
Phone
Birthday
Special Requirements

Notes

Name	Date	Time	Service	Price

Address

Email
Phone
Birthday
Special Requirements

Notes

E

Name	Appointments			
	Date	Time	Service	Price
Address				
Email				
Phone				
Birthday				
Special Requirements				
Notes				

Name	Date	Time	Service	Price
Address				
Email				
Phone				
Birthday				
Special Requirements				
Notes				

E

	Appointments			
Name	Date	Time	Service	Price
Address				
Email				
Phone				
Birthday				
Special Requirements				
Notes				

Name	Date	Time	Service	Price
Address				
Email				
Phone				
Birthday				
Special Requirements				
Notes				

E

Name	Appointments			
	Date	Time	Service	Price
Address				
Email				
Phone				
Birthday				
Special Requirements				
Notes				

Name	Date	Time	Service	Price
Address				
Email				
Phone				
Birthday				
Special Requirements				
Notes				

E

Name	Appointments			
	Date	Time	Service	Price
Address				
Email				
Phone				
Birthday				
Special Requirements				
Notes				

Name	Date	Time	Service	Price
Address				
Email				
Phone				
Birthday				
Special Requirements				
Notes				

E

Name	Appointments			
	Date	Time	Service	Price
Address				
Email				
Phone				
Birthday				
Special Requirements				
Notes				

Name	Date	Time	Service	Price
Address				
Email				
Phone				
Birthday				
Special Requirements				
Notes				

E

Name	Appointments			
	Date	Time	Service	Price
Address				
Email				
Phone				
Birthday				
Special Requirements				
Notes				

Name	Date	Time	Service	Price
Address				
Email				
Phone				
Birthday				
Special Requirements				
Notes				

F

Name	Appointments			
	Date	Time	Service	Price
Address				
Email				
Phone				
Birthday				
Special Requirements				
Notes				

Name	Date	Time	Service	Price
Address				
Email				
Phone				
Birthday				
Special Requirements				
Notes				

	Appointments			
Name	Date	Time	Service	Price
Address				
Email				
Phone				
Birthday				
Special Requirements				
Notes				
Name	Date	Time	Service	Price
Address				
Email				
Phone				
Birthday				
Special Requirements				
Notes				

F

F

	Appointments			
Name	Date	Time	Service	Price

Address

Email

Phone

Birthday

Special Requirements

Notes

Name	Date	Time	Service	Price

Address

Email

Phone

Birthday

Special Requirements

Notes

F

Name	Appointments			
	Date	Time	Service	Price
Address				
Email				
Phone				
Birthday				
Special Requirements				
Notes				

Name	Date	Time	Service	Price
Address				
Email				
Phone				
Birthday				
Special Requirements				
Notes				

F

Name	Appointments			
	Date	Time	Service	Price
Address				
Email				
Phone				
Birthday				
Special Requirements				
Notes				

Name	Date	Time	Service	Price
Address				
Email				
Phone				
Birthday				
Special Requirements				
Notes				

F

	Appointments			
Name	Date	Time	Service	Price
Address				
Email				
Phone				
Birthday				
Special Requirements				
Notes				
Name	Date	Time	Service	Price
Address				
Email				
Phone				
Birthday				
Special Requirements				
Notes				

G

	Appointments			
Name	**Date**	**Time**	**Service**	**Price**

Address

Email
Phone
Birthday
Special Requirements

Notes

Name	**Date**	**Time**	**Service**	**Price**

Address

Email
Phone
Birthday
Special Requirements

Notes

G

Name	Appointments			
	Date	Time	Service	Price
Address				
Email				
Phone				
Birthday				
Special Requirements				
Notes				

Name	Date	Time	Service	Price
Address				
Email				
Phone				
Birthday				
Special Requirements				
Notes				

G

Name	Appointments			
	Date	Time	Service	Price
Address				
Email				
Phone				
Birthday				
Special Requirements				
Notes				

Name	Date	Time	Service	Price
Address				
Email				
Phone				
Birthday				
Special Requirements				
Notes				

G

Name	Appointments			
	Date	Time	Service	Price
Address				
Email				
Phone				
Birthday				
Special Requirements				
Notes				

Name	Date	Time	Service	Price
Address				
Email				
Phone				
Birthday				
Special Requirements				
Notes				

G

Name		Appointments		
	Date	Time	Service	Price
Address				
Email				
Phone				
Birthday				
Special Requirements				
Notes				

Name	Date	Time	Service	Price
Address				
Email				
Phone				
Birthday				
Special Requirements				
Notes				

G

Name	Appointments			
	Date	Time	Service	Price

Address

Email
Phone
Birthday
Special Requirements

Notes

Name	Date	Time	Service	Price

Address

Email
Phone
Birthday
Special Requirements

Notes

H

Name	Appointments			
	Date	Time	Service	Price
Address				
Email				
Phone				
Birthday				
Special Requirements				
Notes				

Name	Date	Time	Service	Price
Address				
Email				
Phone				
Birthday				
Special Requirements				
Notes				

H

Name	Appointments			
	Date	Time	Service	Price
Address				
Email				
Phone				
Birthday				
Special Requirements				
Notes				

Name	Date	Time	Service	Price
Address				
Email				
Phone				
Birthday				
Special Requirements				
Notes				

H

Name	Appointments			
	Date	Time	Service	Price
Address				
Email				
Phone				
Birthday				
Special Requirements				
Notes				

Name	Date	Time	Service	Price
Address				
Email				
Phone				
Birthday				
Special Requirements				
Notes				

Name	Appointments			
	Date	Time	Service	Price
Address				
Email				
Phone				
Birthday				
Special Requirements				
Notes				

Name	Date	Time	Service	Price
Address				
Email				
Phone				
Birthday				
Special Requirements				
Notes				

H

Name	Appointments			
	Date	Time	Service	Price
Address				
Email				
Phone				
Birthday				
Special Requirements				
Notes				

Name	Date	Time	Service	Price
Address				
Email				
Phone				
Birthday				
Special Requirements				
Notes				

H

Name	Appointments			
	Date	Time	Service	Price
Address				
Email				
Phone				
Birthday				
Special Requirements				
Notes				

Name	Date	Time	Service	Price
Address				
Email				
Phone				
Birthday				
Special Requirements				
Notes				

I

Name		Appointments		
	Date	Time	Service	Price
Address				
Email				
Phone				
Birthday				
Special Requirements				
Notes				

Name	Date	Time	Service	Price
Address				
Email				
Phone				
Birthday				
Special Requirements				
Notes				

Name	Appointments			
	Date	Time	Service	Price
Address				
Email				
Phone				
Birthday				
Special Requirements				
Notes				

Name	Date	Time	Service	Price
Address				
Email				
Phone				
Birthday				
Special Requirements				
Notes				

I

Name	Appointments			
	Date	Time	Service	Price
Address				
Email				
Phone				
Birthday				
Special Requirements				
Notes				

Name	Date	Time	Service	Price
Address				
Email				
Phone				
Birthday				
Special Requirements				
Notes				

	Appointments			
Name	Date	Time	Service	Price
Address				
Email				
Phone				
Birthday				
Special Requirements				
Notes				

Name	Date	Time	Service	Price
Address				
Email				
Phone				
Birthday				
Special Requirements				
Notes				

Name		Appointments		
	Date	Time	Service	Price
Address				
Email				
Phone				
Birthday				
Special Requirements				
Notes				

Name	Date	Time	Service	Price
Address				
Email				
Phone				
Birthday				
Special Requirements				
Notes				

	Appointments			
Name	Date	Time	Service	Price
Address				
Email				
Phone				
Birthday				
Special Requirements				
Notes				

Name	Date	Time	Service	Price
Address				
Email				
Phone				
Birthday				
Special Requirements				
Notes				

J

Name	Appointments			
	Date	Time	Service	Price
Address				
Email				
Phone				
Birthday				
Special Requirements				
Notes				

Name	Date	Time	Service	Price
Address				
Email				
Phone				
Birthday				
Special Requirements				
Notes				

J

Name	Appointments			
	Date	Time	Service	Price
Address				
Email				
Phone				
Birthday				
Special Requirements				
Notes				

Name	Date	Time	Service	Price
Address				
Email				
Phone				
Birthday				
Special Requirements				
Notes				

J

	Appointments			
Name	Date	Time	Service	Price
Address				
Email				
Phone				
Birthday				
Special Requirements				
Notes				

Name	Date	Time	Service	Price
Address				
Email				
Phone				
Birthday				
Special Requirements				
Notes				

J

Name	Appointments			
	Date	Time	Service	Price
Address				
Email				
Phone				
Birthday				
Special Requirements				
Notes				

Name	Date	Time	Service	Price
Address				
Email				
Phone				
Birthday				
Special Requirements				
Notes				

J

Name	Appointments			
	Date	Time	Service	Price
Address				
Email				
Phone				
Birthday				
Special Requirements				
Notes				

Name				
	Date	Time	Service	Price
Address				
Email				
Phone				
Birthday				
Special Requirements				
Notes				

J

Name	Appointments			
	Date	Time	Service	Price
Address				
Email				
Phone				
Birthday				
Special Requirements				
Notes				

Name	Date	Time	Service	Price
Address				
Email				
Phone				
Birthday				
Special Requirements				
Notes				

K

Name	Appointments			
	Date	Time	Service	Price
Address				
Email				
Phone				
Birthday				
Special Requirements				
Notes				

Name	Date	Time	Service	Price
Address				
Email				
Phone				
Birthday				
Special Requirements				
Notes				

K

Name	Appointments			
	Date	Time	Service	Price
Address				
Email				
Phone				
Birthday				
Special Requirements				
Notes				

Name	Date	Time	Service	Price
Address				
Email				
Phone				
Birthday				
Special Requirements				
Notes				

K

Name	Appointments			
	Date	Time	Service	Price
Address				
Email				
Phone				
Birthday				
Special Requirements				
Notes				

Name	Date	Time	Service	Price
Address				
Email				
Phone				
Birthday				
Special Requirements				
Notes				

K

Name	Appointments			
	Date	Time	Service	Price
Address				
Email				
Phone				
Birthday				
Special Requirements				
Notes				

Name	Date	Time	Service	Price
Address				
Email				
Phone				
Birthday				
Special Requirements				
Notes				

K

Name	Appointments			
	Date	Time	Service	Price
Address				
Email				
Phone				
Birthday				
Special Requirements				
Notes				

Name	Date	Time	Service	Price
Address				
Email				
Phone				
Birthday				
Special Requirements				
Notes				

K

	Appointments			
Name	Date	Time	Service	Price
Address				
Email				
Phone				
Birthday				
Special Requirements				
Notes				
Name	Date	Time	Service	Price
Address				
Email				
Phone				
Birthday				
Special Requirements				
Notes				

L

Name	Appointments			
	Date	Time	Service	Price
Address				
Email				
Phone				
Birthday				
Special Requirements				
Notes				

Name	Date	Time	Service	Price
Address				
Email				
Phone				
Birthday				
Special Requirements				
Notes				

L

Name	Appointments			
	Date	Time	Service	Price
Address				
Email				
Phone				
Birthday				
Special Requirements				
Notes				

Name	Date	Time	Service	Price
Address				
Email				
Phone				
Birthday				
Special Requirements				
Notes				

L

Name	Appointments			
	Date	Time	Service	Price
Address				
Email				
Phone				
Birthday				
Special Requirements				
Notes				

Name	Date	Time	Service	Price
Address				
Email				
Phone				
Birthday				
Special Requirements				
Notes				

L

Name	Appointments			
	Date	Time	Service	Price
Address				
Email				
Phone				
Birthday				
Special Requirements				
Notes				

Name	Date	Time	Service	Price
Address				
Email				
Phone				
Birthday				
Special Requirements				
Notes				

L

Name	Appointments			
	Date	Time	Service	Price
Address				
Email				
Phone				
Birthday				
Special Requirements				
Notes				
Name	Date	Time	Service	Price
Address				
Email				
Phone				
Birthday				
Special Requirements				
Notes				

L

Name	Appointments			
	Date	Time	Service	Price
Address				
Email				
Phone				
Birthday				
Special Requirements				
Notes				

Name	Date	Time	Service	Price
Address				
Email				
Phone				
Birthday				
Special Requirements				
Notes				

M

Name	Appointments			
	Date	Time	Service	Price
Address				
Email				
Phone				
Birthday				
Special Requirements				
Notes				

Name	Date	Time	Service	Price
Address				
Email				
Phone				
Birthday				
Special Requirements				
Notes				

Name	Appointments			
	Date	Time	Service	Price
Address				
Email				
Phone				
Birthday				
Special Requirements				
Notes				

Name	Date	Time	Service	Price
Address				
Email				
Phone				
Birthday				
Special Requirements				
Notes				

Name			Appointments		
		Date	Time	Service	Price
Address					
Email					
Phone					
Birthday					
Special Requirements					
Notes					

Name		Date	Time	Service	Price
Address					
Email					
Phone					
Birthday					
Special Requirements					
Notes					

	Appointments			
Name	Date	Time	Service	Price
Address				
Email				
Phone				
Birthday				
Special Requirements				
Notes				

Name	Date	Time	Service	Price
Address				
Email				
Phone				
Birthday				
Special Requirements				
Notes				

M

Name		Appointments			
		Date	Time	Service	Price
Address					
Email					
Phone					
Birthday					
Special Requirements					
Notes					

Name	Date	Time	Service	Price
Address				
Email				
Phone				
Birthday				
Special Requirements				
Notes				

	Appointments			
Name	Date	Time	Service	Price
Address				
Email				
Phone				
Birthday				
Special Requirements				
Notes				

Name	Date	Time	Service	Price
Address				
Email				
Phone				
Birthday				
Special Requirements				
Notes				

N

Name		Appointments			
		Date	Time	Service	Price
Address					
Email					
Phone					
Birthday					
Special Requirements					
Notes					

Name		Date	Time	Service	Price
Address					
Email					
Phone					
Birthday					
Special Requirements					
Notes					

N

	Appointments			
Name	Date	Time	Service	Price
Address				
Email				
Phone				
Birthday				
Special Requirements				
Notes				

Name	Date	Time	Service	Price
Address				
Email				
Phone				
Birthday				
Special Requirements				
Notes				

N

Name	Appointments			
	Date	Time	Service	Price
Address				
Email				
Phone				
Birthday				
Special Requirements				
Notes				

Name	Date	Time	Service	Price
Address				
Email				
Phone				
Birthday				
Special Requirements				
Notes				

N

Name	Appointments			
	Date	Time	Service	Price
Address				
Email				
Phone				
Birthday				
Special Requirements				
Notes				

Name	Date	Time	Service	Price
Address				
Email				
Phone				
Birthday				
Special Requirements				
Notes				

N

Name	Appointments			
	Date	Time	Service	Price
Address				
Email				
Phone				
Birthday				
Special Requirements				
Notes				

Name	Date	Time	Service	Price
Address				
Email				
Phone				
Birthday				
Special Requirements				
Notes				

N

Name	Appointments			
	Date	Time	Service	Price
Address				
Email				
Phone				
Birthday				
Special Requirements				
Notes				

Name	Date	Time	Service	Price
Address				
Email				
Phone				
Birthday				
Special Requirements				
Notes				

O

Name	Appointments			
	Date	Time	Service	Price
Address				
Email				
Phone				
Birthday				
Special Requirements				
Notes				

Name	Date	Time	Service	Price
Address				
Email				
Phone				
Birthday				
Special Requirements				
Notes				

O

Name	Appointments			
	Date	Time	Service	Price
Address				
Email				
Phone				
Birthday				
Special Requirements				
Notes				

Name	Date	Time	Service	Price
Address				
Email				
Phone				
Birthday				
Special Requirements				
Notes				

O

Name	Appointments			
	Date	Time	Service	Price
Address				
Email				
Phone				
Birthday				
Special Requirements				
Notes				

Name				
	Date	Time	Service	Price
Address				
Email				
Phone				
Birthday				
Special Requirements				
Notes				

O

Name	Appointments			
	Date	Time	Service	Price
Address				
Email				
Phone				
Birthday				
Special Requirements				
Notes				

Name	Date	Time	Service	Price
Address				
Email				
Phone				
Birthday				
Special Requirements				
Notes				

O

Name	Appointments			
	Date	Time	Service	Price
Address				
Email				
Phone				
Birthday				
Special Requirements				
Notes				

Name				
	Date	Time	Service	Price
Address				
Email				
Phone				
Birthday				
Special Requirements				
Notes				

O

Name	Appointments			
	Date	Time	Service	Price
Address				
Email				
Phone				
Birthday				
Special Requirements				
Notes				

Name	Date	Time	Service	Price
Address				
Email				
Phone				
Birthday				
Special Requirements				
Notes				

P

	Appointments			
Name	Date	Time	Service	Price
Address				
Email				
Phone				
Birthday				
Special Requirements				
Notes				

Name	Date	Time	Service	Price
Address				
Email				
Phone				
Birthday				
Special Requirements				
Notes				

P

Name	Appointments			
	Date	Time	Service	Price
Address				
Email				
Phone				
Birthday				
Special Requirements				
Notes				

Name	Date	Time	Service	Price
Address				
Email				
Phone				
Birthday				
Special Requirements				
Notes				

P

Name	Appointments			
	Date	Time	Service	Price
Address				
Email				
Phone				
Birthday				
Special Requirements				
Notes				

Name	Date	Time	Service	Price
Address				
Email				
Phone				
Birthday				
Special Requirements				
Notes				

P

Name	Appointments			
	Date	Time	Service	Price

Address

Email
Phone
Birthday
Special Requirements

Notes

Name	Date	Time	Service	Price

Address

Email
Phone
Birthday
Special Requirements

Notes

P

Name	Appointments			
	Date	Time	Service	Price
Address				
Email				
Phone				
Birthday				
Special Requirements				
Notes				

Name	Date	Time	Service	Price
Address				
Email				
Phone				
Birthday				
Special Requirements				
Notes				

P

Name	Appointments			
	Date	Time	Service	Price
Address				
Email				
Phone				
Birthday				
Special Requirements				
Notes				

Name	Date	Time	Service	Price
Address				
Email				
Phone				
Birthday				
Special Requirements				
Notes				

Q

Name		Appointments			
		Date	Time	Service	Price
Address					
Email					
Phone					
Birthday					
Special Requirements					
Notes					

Name		Date	Time	Service	Price
Address					
Email					
Phone					
Birthday					
Special Requirements					
Notes					

Q

Name	Appointments			
	Date	Time	Service	Price

Address

Email
Phone
Birthday
Special Requirements

Notes

Name	Date	Time	Service	Price

Address

Email
Phone
Birthday
Special Requirements

Notes

Q

Name	Appointments			
	Date	Time	Service	Price
Address				
Email				
Phone				
Birthday				
Special Requirements				
Notes				

Name	Date	Time	Service	Price
Address				
Email				
Phone				
Birthday				
Special Requirements				
Notes				

Q

	Appointments			
Name	Date	Time	Service	Price
Address				
Email				
Phone				
Birthday				
Special Requirements				
Notes				

Name	Date	Time	Service	Price
Address				
Email				
Phone				
Birthday				
Special Requirements				
Notes				

Q

Name	Appointments			
	Date	Time	Service	Price
Address				
Email				
Phone				
Birthday				
Special Requirements				
Notes				

Name	Date	Time	Service	Price
Address				
Email				
Phone				
Birthday				
Special Requirements				
Notes				

Q

Name	Appointments			
	Date	Time	Service	Price
Address				
Email				
Phone				
Birthday				
Special Requirements				
Notes				

Name	Date	Time	Service	Price
Address				
Email				
Phone				
Birthday				
Special Requirements				
Notes				

R

Name	Appointments			
	Date	Time	Service	Price
Address				
Email				
Phone				
Birthday				
Special Requirements				
Notes				

Name	Date	Time	Service	Price
Address				
Email				
Phone				
Birthday				
Special Requirements				
Notes				

R

Name	Appointments			
	Date	Time	Service	Price
Address				
Email				
Phone				
Birthday				
Special Requirements				
Notes				

Name	Date	Time	Service	Price
Address				
Email				
Phone				
Birthday				
Special Requirements				
Notes				

R

	Appointments			
Name	Date	Time	Service	Price
Address				
Email				
Phone				
Birthday				
Special Requirements				
Notes				

Name	Date	Time	Service	Price
Address				
Email				
Phone				
Birthday				
Special Requirements				
Notes				

R

Name	Appointments			
	Date	Time	Service	Price
Address				
Email				
Phone				
Birthday				
Special Requirements				
Notes				

Name	Date	Time	Service	Price
Address				
Email				
Phone				
Birthday				
Special Requirements				
Notes				

R

Name	Appointments			
	Date	Time	Service	Price
Address				
Email				
Phone				
Birthday				
Special Requirements				
Notes				

Name	Date	Time	Service	Price
Address				
Email				
Phone				
Birthday				
Special Requirements				
Notes				

R

Name	Appointments			
	Date	Time	Service	Price
Address				
Email				
Phone				
Birthday				
Special Requirements				
Notes				

Name	Date	Time	Service	Price
Address				
Email				
Phone				
Birthday				
Special Requirements				
Notes				

S

	Appointments			
Name	Date	Time	Service	Price
Address				
Email				
Phone				
Birthday				
Special Requirements				
Notes				

Name	Date	Time	Service	Price
Address				
Email				
Phone				
Birthday				
Special Requirements				
Notes				

S

Name	Appointments			
	Date	Time	Service	Price
Address				
Email				
Phone				
Birthday				
Special Requirements				
Notes				

Name	Date	Time	Service	Price
Address				
Email				
Phone				
Birthday				
Special Requirements				
Notes				

S

Name	Appointments			
	Date	Time	Service	Price
Address				
Email				
Phone				
Birthday				
Special Requirements				
Notes				

Name	Date	Time	Service	Price
Address				
Email				
Phone				
Birthday				
Special Requirements				
Notes				

S

Name	Appointments			
	Date	Time	Service	Price
Address				
Email				
Phone				
Birthday				
Special Requirements				
Notes				

Name	Date	Time	Service	Price
Address				
Email				
Phone				
Birthday				
Special Requirements				
Notes				

S

Name	Appointments			
	Date	Time	Service	Price

Address

Email
Phone
Birthday
Special Requirements

Notes

Name	Date	Time	Service	Price

Address

Email
Phone
Birthday
Special Requirements

Notes

S

Name	Appointments			
	Date	Time	Service	Price
Address				
Email				
Phone				
Birthday				
Special Requirements				
Notes				

Name	Date	Time	Service	Price
Address				
Email				
Phone				
Birthday				
Special Requirements				
Notes				

T

Name	Appointments			
	Date	Time	Service	Price
Address				
Email				
Phone				
Birthday				
Special Requirements				
Notes				

Name	Date	Time	Service	Price
Address				
Email				
Phone				
Birthday				
Special Requirements				
Notes				

T

Name	Appointments			
	Date	Time	Service	Price
Address				
Email				
Phone				
Birthday				
Special Requirements				
Notes				

Name	Date	Time	Service	Price
Address				
Email				
Phone				
Birthday				
Special Requirements				
Notes				

T

Name	Appointments			
	Date	Time	Service	Price
Address				
Email				
Phone				
Birthday				
Special Requirements				
Notes				

Name				
	Date	Time	Service	Price
Address				
Email				
Phone				
Birthday				
Special Requirements				
Notes				

T

Name	Appointments			
	Date	Time	Service	Price
Address				
Email				
Phone				
Birthday				
Special Requirements				
Notes				

Name	Date	Time	Service	Price
Address				
Email				
Phone				
Birthday				
Special Requirements				
Notes				

T

Name	Appointments			
	Date	Time	Service	Price
Address				
Email				
Phone				
Birthday				
Special Requirements				
Notes				

Name	Date	Time	Service	Price
Address				
Email				
Phone				
Birthday				
Special Requirements				
Notes				

T

Name	Appointments			
	Date	Time	Service	Price
Address				
Email				
Phone				
Birthday				
Special Requirements				
Notes				

Name	Date	Time	Service	Price
Address				
Email				
Phone				
Birthday				
Special Requirements				
Notes				

U

Name	Appointments			
	Date	Time	Service	Price
Address				
Email				
Phone				
Birthday				
Special Requirements				
Notes				

Name	Date	Time	Service	Price
Address				
Email				
Phone				
Birthday				
Special Requirements				
Notes				

U

Name	Appointments			
	Date	Time	Service	Price
Address				
Email				
Phone				
Birthday				
Special Requirements				
Notes				

Name	Date	Time	Service	Price
Address				
Email				
Phone				
Birthday				
Special Requirements				
Notes				

U

	Appointments			
Name	Date	Time	Service	Price
Address				
Email				
Phone				
Birthday				
Special Requirements				
Notes				

Name	Date	Time	Service	Price
Address				
Email				
Phone				
Birthday				
Special Requirements				
Notes				

U

Name	Appointments			
	Date	Time	Service	Price
Address				
Email				
Phone				
Birthday				
Special Requirements				
Notes				

Name	Date	Time	Service	Price
Address				
Email				
Phone				
Birthday				
Special Requirements				
Notes				

U

Name	Appointments			
	Date	Time	Service	Price
Address				
Email				
Phone				
Birthday				
Special Requirements				
Notes				

Name	Date	Time	Service	Price
Address				
Email				
Phone				
Birthday				
Special Requirements				
Notes				

U

Name	Appointments			
	Date	Time	Service	Price
Address				
Email				
Phone				
Birthday				
Special Requirements				
Notes				

Name	Date	Time	Service	Price
Address				
Email				
Phone				
Birthday				
Special Requirements				
Notes				

V

Name	Appointments			
	Date	Time	Service	Price
Address				
Email				
Phone				
Birthday				
Special Requirements				
Notes				

Name	Appointments			
	Date	Time	Service	Price
Address				
Email				
Phone				
Birthday				
Special Requirements				
Notes				

V

| Name | Appointments ||||
	Date	Time	Service	Price
Address				
Email				
Phone				
Birthday				
Special Requirements				
Notes				

Name	Date	Time	Service	Price
Address				
Email				
Phone				
Birthday				
Special Requirements				
Notes				

V

Name	Appointments			
	Date	Time	Service	Price
Address				
Email				
Phone				
Birthday				
Special Requirements				
Notes				

Name	Date	Time	Service	Price
Address				
Email				
Phone				
Birthday				
Special Requirements				
Notes				

V

Name	Appointments			
	Date	Time	Service	Price
Address				
Email				
Phone				
Birthday				
Special Requirements				
Notes				

Name	Date	Time	Service	Price
Address				
Email				
Phone				
Birthday				
Special Requirements				
Notes				

V

Name	Appointments			
	Date	Time	Service	Price
Address				
Email				
Phone				
Birthday				
Special Requirements				
Notes				

Name	Date	Time	Service	Price
Address				
Email				
Phone				
Birthday				
Special Requirements				
Notes				

V

Name	Appointments			
	Date	Time	Service	Price
Address				
Email				
Phone				
Birthday				
Special Requirements				
Notes				

Name	Date	Time	Service	Price
Address				
Email				
Phone				
Birthday				
Special Requirements				
Notes				

Name		Appointments		
	Date	Time	Service	Price
Address				
Email				
Phone				
Birthday				
Special Requirements				
Notes				

Name	Date	Time	Service	Price
Address				
Email				
Phone				
Birthday				
Special Requirements				
Notes				

W

Name	Appointments			
	Date	Time	Service	Price
Address				
Email				
Phone				
Birthday				
Special Requirements				
Notes				

Name	Date	Time	Service	Price
Address				
Email				
Phone				
Birthday				
Special Requirements				
Notes				

Name		Appointments		
	Date	Time	Service	Price
Address				
Email				
Phone				
Birthday				
Special Requirements				
Notes				

Name	Date	Time	Service	Price
Address				
Email				
Phone				
Birthday				
Special Requirements				
Notes				

W

	Appointments			
Name	Date	Time	Service	Price

Address

Email
Phone
Birthday
Special Requirements

Notes

Name	Date	Time	Service	Price

Address

Email
Phone
Birthday
Special Requirements

Notes

Name	Appointments			
	Date	Time	Service	Price
Address				
Email				
Phone				
Birthday				
Special Requirements				
Notes				

Name	Date	Time	Service	Price
Address				
Email				
Phone				
Birthday				
Special Requirements				
Notes				

W

Name	Appointments			
	Date	Time	Service	Price
Address				
Email				
Phone				
Birthday				
Special Requirements				
Notes				

Name	Date	Time	Service	Price
Address				
Email				
Phone				
Birthday				
Special Requirements				
Notes				

X

Name	Appointments			
	Date	Time	Service	Price
Address				
Email				
Phone				
Birthday				
Special Requirements				
Notes				

Name	Date	Time	Service	Price
Address				
Email				
Phone				
Birthday				
Special Requirements				
Notes				

X

Name	Appointments			
	Date	Time	Service	Price
Address				
Email				
Phone				
Birthday				
Special Requirements				
Notes				

Name	Date	Time	Service	Price
Address				
Email				
Phone				
Birthday				
Special Requirements				
Notes				

Name		Appointments			
		Date	Time	Service	Price
Address					
Email					
Phone					
Birthday					
Special Requirements					
Notes					

Name		Date	Time	Service	Price
Address					
Email					
Phone					
Birthday					
Special Requirements					
Notes					

Name	Appointments			
	Date	Time	Service	Price
Address				
Email				
Phone				
Birthday				
Special Requirements				
Notes				

Name	Date	Time	Service	Price
Address				
Email				
Phone				
Birthday				
Special Requirements				
Notes				

Name	Appointments			
	Date	Time	Service	Price
Address				
Email				
Phone				
Birthday				
Special Requirements				
Notes				

Name	Date	Time	Service	Price
Address				
Email				
Phone				
Birthday				
Special Requirements				
Notes				

X

	Appointments			
Name	Date	Time	Service	Price
Address				
Email				
Phone				
Birthday				
Special Requirements				
Notes				
Name	Date	Time	Service	Price
Address				
Email				
Phone				
Birthday				
Special Requirements				
Notes				

Y

Name	Appointments			
	Date	Time	Service	Price
Address				
Email				
Phone				
Birthday				
Special Requirements				
Notes				

Name	Date	Time	Service	Price
Address				
Email				
Phone				
Birthday				
Special Requirements				
Notes				

Y

Name	Appointments			
	Date	Time	Service	Price
Address				
Email				
Phone				
Birthday				
Special Requirements				
Notes				

Name	Date	Time	Service	Price
Address				
Email				
Phone				
Birthday				
Special Requirements				
Notes				

Y

Name	Appointments			
	Date	Time	Service	Price
Address				
Email				
Phone				
Birthday				
Special Requirements				
Notes				

Name	Date	Time	Service	Price
Address				
Email				
Phone				
Birthday				
Special Requirements				
Notes				

Y

Name	Appointments			
	Date	Time	Service	Price
Address				
Email				
Phone				
Birthday				
Special Requirements				
Notes				

Name	Date	Time	Service	Price
Address				
Email				
Phone				
Birthday				
Special Requirements				
Notes				

Y

Name	Appointments			
	Date	Time	Service	Price
Address				
Email				
Phone				
Birthday				
Special Requirements				
Notes				

Name	Date	Time	Service	Price
Address				
Email				
Phone				
Birthday				
Special Requirements				
Notes				

Y

Name	Appointments			
	Date	Time	Service	Price
Address				
Email				
Phone				
Birthday				
Special Requirements				
Notes				

Name	Date	Time	Service	Price
Address				
Email				
Phone				
Birthday				
Special Requirements				
Notes				

Z

Name	Appointments			
	Date	Time	Service	Price
Address				
Email				
Phone				
Birthday				
Special Requirements				
Notes				

Name	Appointments			
	Date	Time	Service	Price
Address				
Email				
Phone				
Birthday				
Special Requirements				
Notes				

Z

Name	Appointments			
	Date	Time	Service	Price
Address				
Email				
Phone				
Birthday				
Special Requirements				
Notes				

Name	Date	Time	Service	Price
Address				
Email				
Phone				
Birthday				
Special Requirements				
Notes				

Z

Name	Appointments			
	Date	Time	Service	Price
Address				
Email				
Phone				
Birthday				
Special Requirements				
Notes				

Name	Date	Time	Service	Price
Address				
Email				
Phone				
Birthday				
Special Requirements				
Notes				

Z

	Appointments			
Name	Date	Time	Service	Price
Address				
Email				
Phone				
Birthday				
Special Requirements				
Notes				

Name	Date	Time	Service	Price
Address				
Email				
Phone				
Birthday				
Special Requirements				
Notes				

Z

Name	Appointments			
	Date	Time	Service	Price
Address				
Email				
Phone				
Birthday				
Special Requirements				
Notes				

Name	Date	Time	Service	Price
Address				
Email				
Phone				
Birthday				
Special Requirements				
Notes				

Z

	Appointments			
Name	Date	Time	Service	Price
Address				
Email				
Phone				
Birthday				
Special Requirements				
Notes				
Name	Date	Time	Service	Price
Address				
Email				
Phone				
Birthday				
Special Requirements				
Notes				

Hints: May 27th

Made in the USA
Las Vegas, NV
05 April 2023